REMARKABLE

PEOPLE

Sandra Day O'Connor

by Jennifer Howse

Published by Weigl Publishers Inc.
350 5th Avenue, Suite 3304, PMB 6G
New York, NY 10118-0069

Website: www.weigl.com
Copyright ©2008 WEIGL PUBLISHERS INC.

Library of Congress Cataloging-in-Publication Data

Howse, Jennifer.
 Sandra Day O'Connor / Jennifer Howse.
    p. cm. -- (Remarkable people)
 Includes index.
 ISBN 978-1-59036-647-9 (hard cover : alk. paper) -- ISBN 978-1-59036-648-6 (soft
cover : alk. paper)
 1. O'Connor, Sandra Day 1930---Juvenile literature. 2. Judges--United States--
Biography--Juvenile literature. 3. United States. Supreme Court--Biography--
Juvenile literature. I. Title.
 KF8745.O25H68 2008
 347.73'2634--dc22
 [B]

                        2006039441

Printed in the United States of America
1 2 3 4 5 6 7 8 9 0 11 10 09 08 07

Editor: Leia Tait
Design: Terry Paulhus

Cover: Sandra's success has inspired many other women to achieve great things.

Photograph Credits
Collection of the Supreme Court of the United States: pages 6, 8, 10; Permission to
use granted by the Office of the Secretary of State of Arizona: page 7 top left.

Contents

Who Is Sandra Day O'Connor?

Sandra Day O'Connor was the first woman to serve as a **judge** in the U.S. **Supreme Court**. Sandra served as a Supreme Court judge from 1981 to 2006. During that time, Sandra made many important decisions about the law. She worked to make sure all people in the United States receive fair treatment in court. She set an example of good **citizenship**. Thoughout her life, Sandra has acted with courage and wisdom to achieve great things. She continues to be an example for people of all ages.

"Each one of us will be a leader at some time in our lives."

Growing Up

Sandra Day O'Connor was born March 26, 1930, to Harry Day and Ada Mae Wilkey Day. Sandra was an only child until she was eight. That year, her younger sister, Ann, was born. Her brother Alan was born the following year. The family lived on a cattle ranch near Duncan, Arizona. It was called the Lazy B Ranch. Sandra's grandfather, Henry Clay Day, built the ranch in the 1880s. On the ranch, Sandra learned how to ride a horse and drive a truck. She performed many chores. These included cooking meals, washing clothes, and mending fences.

During Sandra's early childhood, the United States went through the **Great Depression**. Money was scarce. There was not enough rain for farmers to grow healthy crops. Like many people, Sandra's family faced great hardships during this time. The Great Depression lasted until 1940. During the next few years, the Lazy B Ranch became a thriving business.

■ Sandra enjoyed growing up on the Lazy B Ranch. She especially loved caring for her pet horse, Chico.

Get to Know Arizona

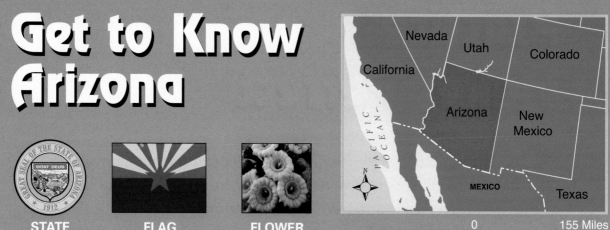

STATE SEAL

FLAG

FLOWER
Saguaro Cactus Blossom

Arizona is bordered by Mexico and the states of California, Nevada, Utah, Colorado, and New Mexico.

More than five million people live in Arizona.

Phoenix is the capital city of Arizona. It is the largest city in the state.

The landscape in southern Arizona is a mix of towering mountains and desert valley.

The ringtail is one of Arizona's official animals. It is named for its bushy, raccoon-like tail.

Think about it!

Arizona is home to people from many different cultural backgrounds. More than one million Hispanic Americans live in the state. About 250,000 American Indians also reside there. How might this **diversity** have influenced Sandra in her career as a judge?

Practice Makes Perfect

The Lazy B Ranch was 25 miles (40 kilometers) from Duncan, the nearest town. It was also very far away from the local public school. At the age of five, Sandra moved to her grandmother's house in El Paso, Texas, so she could attend school. Sandra stayed with her grandmother during the school year. She returned to Lazy B Ranch each summer.

At age 16, Sandra completed her high school diploma in Austin, Texas. She began attending Stanford University in California. There, Sandra studied **economics**. During this time, she discovered that laws can be used to make important changes in society. She wanted to help people who were victims of crimes or who had been treated badly.

■ Sandra learned to read before beginning elementary school.

Once Sandra completed her economics studies in 1950, she decided to become a lawyer. Later that year, Sandra began attending Stanford Law School. She was a good student. In a class of 102 students, Sandra finished third. She earned her law **degree** in June 1952.

Sandra was excited to become a lawyer. She began applying for jobs but was always turned down. **Legal firms** did not want to hire a woman lawyer. At the time, most women in the United States did not work outside the home. Sandra kept trying. She began seeking a job with the government instead of private firms. By the end of 1952, she was working as a lawyer at the San Mateo County Attorney's office.

Many people believe the law program at Stanford University is one of the best in the world.

Key Events

In 1958, Sandra started a law firm with another lawyer, Tom Tobin. Over the next few years, she worked periodically while raising her sons. In 1969, Sandra became a member of the Arizona State **Senate**. She served in the state senate until 1975. During that time, Sandra was chosen to be the senate's **majority leader**. She was the first woman in the United States to earn this title.

Sandra began working as a judge for the Maricopa County Superior Court in 1975. Four years later, she was chosen to serve on the Arizona Court of Appeals. She held that position for two years. In 1981, Sandra experienced a major change in her life. That year, Ronald Reagan was president of the United States. He chose Sandra to be the new judge on the U.S. Supreme Court. She was the first woman to hold such a position.

■ On September 25, 1981, Sandra became the first woman appointed to the U.S. Supreme Court.

Thoughts from Sandra

Sandra often shares her thoughts about her life and the law. Here are some things that she has said.

Sandra believes others have helped her achieve great things.

"We don't accomplish anything in this world alone...and whatever happens is the result of the whole tapestry of one's life and all the weavings of individual threads from one to another that creates something."

Sandra did not always plan to practice law.

"When I was young, I wanted to be a cattle rancher."

Sandra experiences hardship on the Lazy B Ranch during the Great Depression.

"Rain was everything to us. We would look at the sky every day and hope we'd see rain clouds forming. And when they did, we were saved again."

Sandra believes everyone plays an important role in shaping the world.

"Each of us brings to our job, whatever it is, our lifetime of experience and our values."

Sandra becomes the first female Supreme Court judge.

"The power I exert on the court depends on the power of my arguments, not on my gender."

Sandra urges others to take pride in each task they perform.

"Do the best you can in every task, no matter how unimportant it may seem at the time."

What Is a Supreme Court Judge?

A Supreme Court judge is a member of the Supreme Court. The Court is made up of nine judges, who are also called justices. The chief justice leads the Court. All justices are chosen by the president, and must be approved by the U.S. Senate. A Supreme Court judge holds his or her position for life. No new justices can be appointed until one the current nine dies, chooses to give up the position, or is forced to quit by the Senate.

Supreme Court judges must be trained in the law. It is their job to decide some of the most important legal cases in the country. These cases concern the U.S. **Constitution**. Supreme Court justices decide if a law or government action breaks the rules of the Constitution. These decisions can affect the outcome of thousands of cases around the country. For this reason, it is a great responsibility to serve as a Supreme Court judge.

■ At special events, Sandra often meets with other important members of government, including President George W. Bush.

Supreme Court Judges 101

John Jay (1745–1829)

Term: 1789–1795
Achievements: John Jay was the first chief justice of the U.S. Supreme Court. He had previously been a lawyer. He helped end the war between the United States and Great Britain in 1783. In 1789, the U.S. government created the Supreme Court. That year, President George Washington chose Jay to be the Court's first leader. Jay served as chief justice until 1795. He was known for trying to increase the power of the U.S. government over the individual states.

John Marshall (1755–1835)

Term: 1801–1835
Achievements: John Marshall was a soldier who became a lawyer and political figure. In 1801, President John Adams chose Marshall to sit on the Supreme Court. Marshall became the fourth chief justice on January 27 of that year. He held the position for 34 years, longer than anyone else in history. As chief justice, Marshall enforced the Court's right to reverse government laws and actions that broke the laws of the Constitution. This greatly increased the Court's power. Many people believe Marshall was the most important judge in U.S. history.

Thurgood Marshall (1908–1993)

Term: 1967–1991
Achievements: Thurgood Marshall was a well-known lawyer. In 1954, he won a case called *Brown v. Board of Education*. As a result of this case, the Supreme Court found that **segregation** in U.S. schools broke laws written in the Constitution. This helped to end the practice throughout the country. In 1967, President Lyndon B. Johnson chose Marshall to join the Supreme Court. Marshall was the 96th Supreme Court justice and the first African American to hold such a position. He served on the Court for 23 years. During that time, Marshall worked hard to ensure that all people were treated fairly under the law.

Ruth Bader Ginsburg (1933–)

Term: 1993–
Achievements: Before joining the Supreme Court, Ruth Bader Ginsburg was a well-known lawyer and law professor. As a lawyer, she worked to improve women's rights. In the 1970s, Ginsburg led the country-wide Women's Rights Project. In 1972, she was the first woman to become a **tenured** professor at Columbia Law School in New York City. She later served on the U.S. Court of Appeals. In 1993, President Bill Clinton chose Ginsburg to join the Supreme Court. Ginsburg is the second woman to become a Supreme Court judge.

The Gavel

The gavel is a small hammer used by judges in a courtroom. It it used to symbolize that a judge is the leader in the courtroom. The gavel is usually made of wood. At key times during a court case, a judge bangs the gavel on his or her desk, which is called the judge's bench. This action is used to bring order to the courtroom. It is also used to make the final word of the judge official.

Influences

Sandra's father, Harry, was a strong influence in her life. His hard work impressed Sandra. As a young man, Harry took control of the Lazy B Ranch from his father instead of going to university. He struggled for many years to make the ranch a success. In time, the ranch grew. It became the largest and most successful ranch in the area.

Along with Sandra's family, many cowboys worked on the Lazy B Ranch. Since there were no other children nearby, the cowboys were Sandra's closest friends. They had a strong impact on her life. The cowboys taught Sandra many lessons about hard work and responsibility. They taught her to do every task to the best of her abilities. They showed Sandra that she could solve problems on her own.

■ Sandra values her experiences growing up on the Lazy B Ranch. In her office at the Supreme Court, she kept a sign on the wall that said "Cowgirl Parking Only."

As a student, Sandra admired many of her teachers. The teacher who had the most influence on Sandra's life was Dr. Harry J. Ratbun. Dr. Ratbun was a lawyer. He was also a professor at Stanford University. Dr. Ratbun taught his students to explore new ideas. He urged them to respect the law and themselves. Sandra thought Dr. Ratbun was a wonderful teacher. His classes inspired her to attend law school.

Sandra believes she can learn something from everyone she meets, even people she disagrees with. In order to connect with many different people, Sandra has performed **public service** work outside of her legal duties. She has worked for many groups, including the Salvation Army, the Arizona State Hospital, and local schools. As a judge, Sandra drew on these experiences to help decide important cases.

THE SALVATION ARMY

The Salvation Army is a global charity based on **Christian** religious beliefs. It was started in 1865 by William Booth in Great Britain. The Salvation Army aims to meet the basic needs of people around the world. Its members currently work in more than 100 countries. They provide many services to people in need, including shelter, child care, medical care, and education programs. They often work with other charities and government groups. To learn more about the Salvation Army, visit **www.salvationarmy.org**.

■ The Salvation Army is well known for its "bell ringers." Bell ringers ring bells to draw attention to their cause, especially during the holiday season.

Overcoming Obstacles

Sandra is a hopeful person. She keeps a positive attitude when faced with hardship. This has helped her get through many difficult times in her life. When Sandra became a Supreme Court judge, she worried that she was not ready for this important job. She turned to other members of the Court for help. Her fellow justices acted as Sandra's **mentors**. They shared their knowledge and experience with her. Sandra admired them for their ability to share their ideas and influence others in positive ways. To do her best as a judge, Sandra also relied on her own experiences as a rancher and a lawyer. Over time, Sandra became one of the most respected members of the Supreme Court. Some people even called it the "O'Connor Court."

■ Sandra has said she has great respect and affection for the other Supreme Court judges she worked with for so many years.

In 1988, Sandra became ill with breast cancer. The disease changed her life. She felt tired, and she worried about her health. The media reported on her illness constantly. This upset Sandra. She felt her illness was a private issue for herself and her family. Sandra focused on getting well. She had an operation to remove the cancer from her body. It was a success. Sandra was soon healthy again. She was happy to return to her work at the Supreme Court.

In 2005, illness struck Sandra's family again. Her husband, John, became ill with **Alzheimer's disease**. Sandra made a difficult decision. After 24 years as a Supreme Court judge, Sandra decided to retire. She wanted to spend more time with John, her sons, and her grandchildren. On January 31, 2006, Sandra officially retired from the Supreme Court. She was 75 years old.

■ Sandra and John have supported each other through many difficulties during their long marriage.

Achievements and Successes

Throughout her career, Sandra has had many successes. One of the most important has been sharing her knowledge and experiences with others. To do this, Sandra has written many books. The first was called *Lazy B: Growing Up on a Cattle Ranch in the American Southwest*. It was published in 2002. Sandra wrote this book with her brother, Alan. In it, they describe their childhood on the family ranch. In 2005, Sandra wrote a book for children. *Chico* describes her childhood adventures with her pet horse. Sandra has written other books about U.S. law and the Supreme Court, including *The Majesty of the Law*. This book was published in 2003.

■ At special events promoting her books, Sandra often signs copies for her admirers.

Sandra has won many awards during her career. In 2003, she received the Philadelphia Liberty Medal. The medal is given each July 4 to a group or an individual who has made important changes in society. Sandra was the first woman to receive the medal. In 2005, the Creativity Foundation awarded Sandra the Benjamin Franklin Creativity Laureate Prize. This award recognized the opportunities Sandra has created for other women working in the legal profession. On March 6, 2006, Sandra received the first Lifetime Achievement Award from the National Association of Women Judges (NAWJ). The award recognized her life's work as a Supreme Court justice.

THE NATIONAL ASSOCIATION OF WOMEN JUDGES (NAWJ)

The National Association of Women Judges is a U.S. group that works on behalf of women judges. The group works for fairness and equality between men and women in the courts. NAWJ provides women with legal education about important issues. It helps women excel in the court system, especially as judges. Members come from all levels of the legal system. The group provides training opportunities for women judges. It helps women in the legal system make connections with each other. Learn more about NAWJ by visiting their website at **www.nawj.org**.

Write a Biography

A person's life story can be the subject of a book. This kind of book is called a biography. Biographies describe the lives of remarkable people, such as those who have achieved great success or have done important things to help others. These people may be alive today or they may have lived many years ago. Reading a biography can help you learn more about a remarkable person.

At school, you might be asked to write a biography. First, decide who you want to write about. You can choose a legal hero, such as Sandra Day O'Connor, or any other person you find interesting. Then, find out if your library has any books about this person. Learn as much as you can about him or her. Write down the key events in this person's life. What was this person's childhood like? What has he or she accomplished? What are his or her goals? What makes this person special or unusual?

A concept web is a useful research tool. Read the questions in the following concept web. Answer the questions in your notebook. Your answers will help you write your biography.

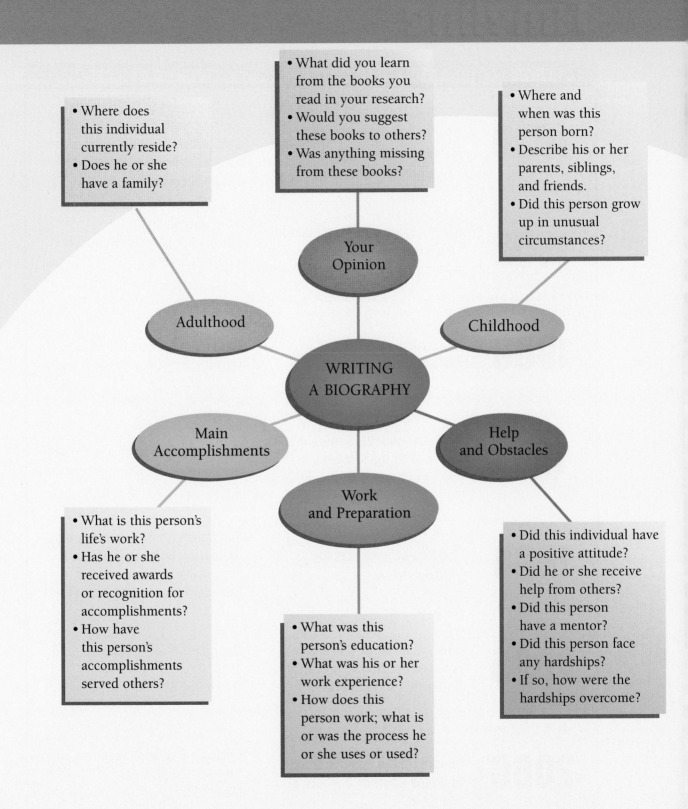

- Where does this individual currently reside?
- Does he or she have a family?

- What did you learn from the books you read in your research?
- Would you suggest these books to others?
- Was anything missing from these books?

- Where and when was this person born?
- Describe his or her parents, siblings, and friends.
- Did this person grow up in unusual circumstances?

Your Opinion

Adulthood

Childhood

WRITING A BIOGRAPHY

Main Accomplishments

Help and Obstacles

Work and Preparation

- What is this person's life's work?
- Has he or she received awards or recognition for accomplishments?
- How have this person's accomplishments served others?

- What was this person's education?
- What was his or her work experience?
- How does this person work; what is or was the process he or she uses or used?

- Did this individual have a positive attitude?
- Did he or she receive help from others?
- Did this person have a mentor?
- Did this person face any hardships?
- If so, how were the hardships overcome?

Timeline

YEAR	SANDRA DAY O'CONNOR	WORLD EVENTS
1930	Sandra is born on March 26 in El Paso, Texas.	On December 2, U.S. President Herbert Hoover requests up to $150 million from the government to create jobs during the Great Depression.
1952	Sandra graduates from Stanford Law School in June. She marries fellow student John Jay O'Connor.	Elizabeth II is crowned queen of Great Britain.
1969	Sandra joins the Arizona State Senate.	Golda Meir becomes the first woman prime minister of Israel.
1981	On September 25, Sandra is sworn in as the first woman justice of the U.S. Supreme Court.	Ronald Reagan becomes the 40th president of the United States.
1988	Sandra becomes ill with breast cancer.	Tun Salleh Abas, lead judge of the Malaysian Supreme Court, is removed from power by Prime Minister Mahathir bin Mohamad.
2005	Sandra publishes *Chico*. She receives the Benjamin Franklin Creativity Laureate Prize.	George W. Bush begins his second term as president of the United States.
2006	Sandra retires from the U.S. Supreme Court on January 31.	Michelle Bachelet becomes the first woman president of Chile on March 11.

Further Research

How can I find out more about Sandra Day O'Connor?

Most libraries have computers that connect to a database for searching for information. If you input a key word, you will be provided with a list of books in the library that contain information on that topic. Non-fiction books are arranged numerically, using their call number. Fiction books are organized alphabetically by the author's last name.

Websites

To learn more about Sandra Day O'Connor, visit
www.supremecourthistory.org
> Click on "History of the Court" and then "Timeline of the Justices" to access a biography of Sandra.

To learn more about the U.S. Supreme Court, visit
www.supremecourtus.gov

Words to Know

Alzheimer's disease: a brain disease that causes memory loss and confusion

Christian: relating to the religion based on the teachings of Jesus Christ

citizenship: membership in society

Constitution: the document containing the basic beliefs, laws, and plan for governing the United States

degree: a title given to a student by a college, university, or professional school upon completion of his or her studies

diversity: great difference or variety

economics: the science that studies how money, goods, and services are produced, distributed, and used

Great Depression: a time during the 1930s when the economy was so poor that many people were unemployed

judge: a person who decides on questions or disagreements in a court of law

legal firms: companies that employ lawyers to represent or give legal advice to clients

majority leader: the person in charge of the party with the most members

mentors: wise and trusted teachers

public service: work done to benefit the public or its institutions

segregation: the practice of setting one racial group apart from another

senate: the law-making branch of government

Supreme Court: the highest court in the United States

tenured: permanently employed

Index